Scott Foresman

Scott Foresman

Editorial Offices: Glenview, Illinois • Parsippany, New Jersey • New York, New York
Sales Offices: Parsippany, New Jersey • Duluth, Georgia • Glenview, Illinois
Coppell, Texas • Ontario, California

Credits

Illustrations

Bill Basso: p. 34; **Maryjane Begin:** cover; **Daniel Del Valle:** pp. 23, 24, 35, 36, 37, 39, 40, 42, 51, 52, 53, 54, 55, 56, 67, 68; **Eldon Doty:** pp. 50, 91; **Ruth J. Flanagan:** pp. 12, 28, 44, 76, 98–108; **Susan T. Hall:** pp. 69, 70, 71, 72, 83, 84, 85, 86, 87, 88, 92; **Olga Jakim:** p. 18; **Kersti Mack:** p. 2; **Patrick Merrell:** pp. 13, 25, 29, 45, 61, 68, 77, 93; **Albert Molnar:** p. 66; **Doug Roy:** pp. 3, 4, 5, 6, 7, 8, 19, 20, 21, 22; **Joanna Roy:** p. 82; **Jessica W. Stanley:** pp. 47, 48, 58, 59, 60, 63, 73, 74, 79, 80, 89, 95, 96; **George Ulrich:** pp. 9, 10, 11, 15, 16, 25, 26, 27, 31, 32, 41, 42, 43

ISBN 0-328-02240-3

ISBN 0-328-04044-4

13 14 15 - VO11 - 10 09 08

14 15 16 17 18 19 - VO11 - 13 12 11 10 09

Table of Contents

Family Times

The Big Mess

The Little Red Hen

Ted Helps

Ted feeds his pet named Ned.
And then he makes his bed.
Ted helps to paint the little shed.
He paints it blue and red.

Ted helps his sister Jen,
Spell words and count to ten.
Ted sets the table. And what then?
He then plays ball with Jen!

This rhyme includes words your child is working with in school: words with the short *e* sound (*pet*, *bed*) and words with double final consonants (*spell*, *ball*). Sing "Ted Helps" with your child. Then work together to draw Ted's pet Ned.

Name: _____

You are your child's first and best teacher!

Here are ways to help your child practice skills while having fun!

Day 1 Write the short *e* word *pet*. Have your child say it. Then, cross out the *p* and add a *b* to make *bet*. Have your child say that word. Continue changing the first letter using *g, j, l, m, n, s, w,* and *y*. List all the short *e* words you make.

Day 2 Write simple sentences using these words that your child is learning to read: *help, now, said, so,* and *who*. Help your child read each sentence aloud.

Day 3 Read aloud one of your child's favorite stories. Have your child tell how the story's characters are alike and how they are different.

Day 4 Your child is learning to read aloud. Read a favorite story together. Ask your child to read the words spoken by the main character, while you read the other parts.

Day 5 Choose a catalog or story with pictures in it. Ask your child to identify any nouns—words that name people, places, animals, and things—shown in the pictures.

Read with your child EVERY DAY!

Cover Up!

Materials paper, marker, bag, 9 buttons per player

Game Directions

1. Use the 18 words below to make 3 X 3 cards like those shown on page 3. Words can be in any order.

2. Write the same 18 words on paper. Cut the words apart and place them in a bag.

3. Players take turns picking a word from the bag and reading it aloud. Players use buttons to cover this word if it is on their cards.

4. The first person to cover three words in a row—across, up, down, or diagonally—wins!

Words

hill, ball, mess, call, doll, bell, yell, kiss, will, miss, tell, sell, bill, wall, pass, tall, fill, fall

ball

sell

miss

hill	call	yell
ball	doll	kiss
mess	bell	will

miss	bill	tall
tell	wall	fill
sell	pass	fall

Circle a word to finish each sentence.
Write it on the line.

hen

pen   pan
_____
- - - - - - - - - -
1. The hen is in the _____ .

pot   pet
_____
- - - - - - - - - -
2. Ken likes to _____ the hen.

bag   beg
_____
- - - - - - - - - -
3. What is in the _____ ?

fed   fan
_____
- - - - - - - - - -
4. The hen wants to be _____ .

miss   mess
_____
- - - - - - - - - -
5. The hen makes a _____ .

Notes for Home: Your child practiced reading and writing words with the short *e* sound heard in h*e*n. **Home Activity:** Work with your child to make a list of all the words on this page with a short *e*.

Name _____

Say the word for each picture.
Circle the letters to finish each word.
Write the letters on the line.

ba<u>ll</u>

1.

all   ell

_____

b _____

2.

ell   all

_____

w _____

3.

oll   ill

_____

d _____

4.

all   ell

_____

c _____

5.

ess   iss

_____

k _____

6.

ell   ill

_____

w _____

7.

all   ell

_____

y _____

8.

ill   all

_____

f _____

9.

ill   all

_____

b _____

10.

oss   ess

_____

m _____

Notes for Home: Your child is learning words with double final consonants *(wall, hill, kiss).*
Home Activity: Have fun taking turns naming words that rhyme with the ones your child
wrote on this page.

Name _____

Pick a word from the box to finish each sentence.
Write it on the line.

help	now	said	so	who

1. _____ _____ can get the cat?

2. Ben can _____ the cat get down.

3. Who can help them _____ ?

4. "Go find Dad!" Ben _____ to Nan.

5. He is here!

_____ now we can get down.

Notes for Home: This week your child is learning to read the words *help, now, said, so,* and *who. Home Activity:* Ask your child to use each word in a spoken sentence.

Look at the picture.

Circle the answer to each question.

Hint: One question will have two answers.

1. Who is little?   Tess   Bess

2. Who is big?   Tess   Bess

3. Who is sitting up?   Tess   Bess

4. Who is sleeping?   Tess   Bess

5. Who is a dog?   Tess   Bess

6. **Draw** two dogs that are the same.

7. **Draw** two dogs that are different.

Notes for Home: Your child compared and contrasted two animal characters. *Home Activity:* Choose two animals that your child likes. Have your child tell how they are alike and different.

Name _____

A **noun** names a person, place, animal, or thing.

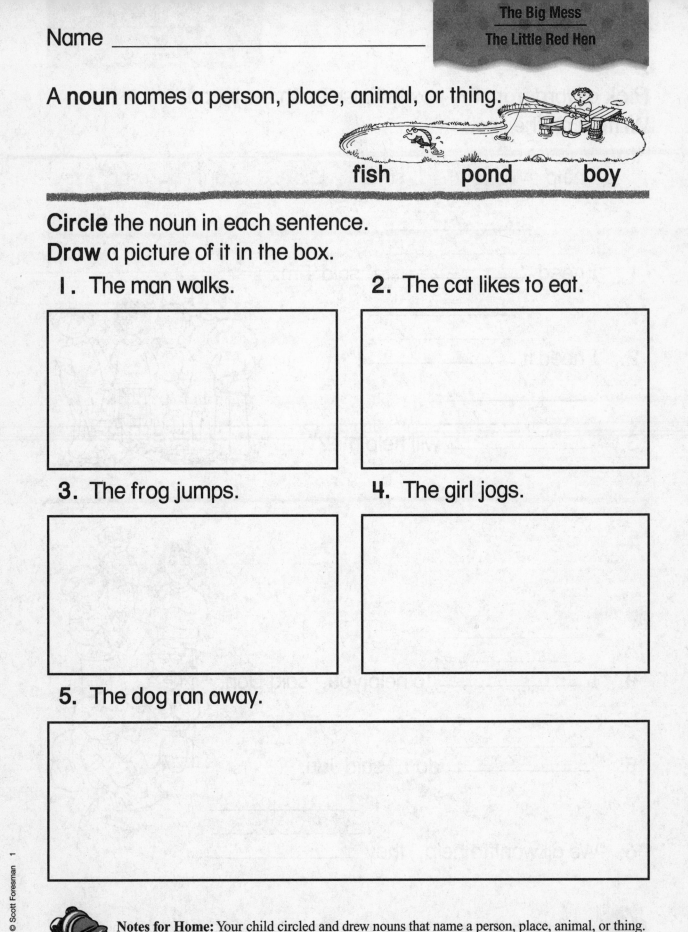

fish   pond   boy

Circle the noun in each sentence.
Draw a picture of it in the box.

1. The man walks.

2. The cat likes to eat.

3. The frog jumps.

4. The girl jogs.

5. The dog ran away.

Notes for Home: Your child circled and drew nouns that name a person, place, animal, or thing. *Home Activity:* Help your child draw and label pictures of people, places, animals, and things that are in or near your home.

Pick a word from the box to finish each sentence.
Write it on the line.

| help | now | said | so | want | who |

1. "I need _____ !" said Tim.

2. "I need it _____ !"

3. "_____ will help me?"

4. "I _____ to help you," said Dan.

5. "_____ do I," said Jan.

6. "We all want to help," they _____ .

Notes for Home: Your child read and wrote the words *help, now, said, so, want,* and *who* to complete sentences. **Home Activity:** Ask your child to use each vocabulary word in a short sentence. Work together to write each sentence.

© Scott Foresman 1

Name _____

Say the word for each picture.
Write o if the word has a **short o** sound.

h<u>o</u>g

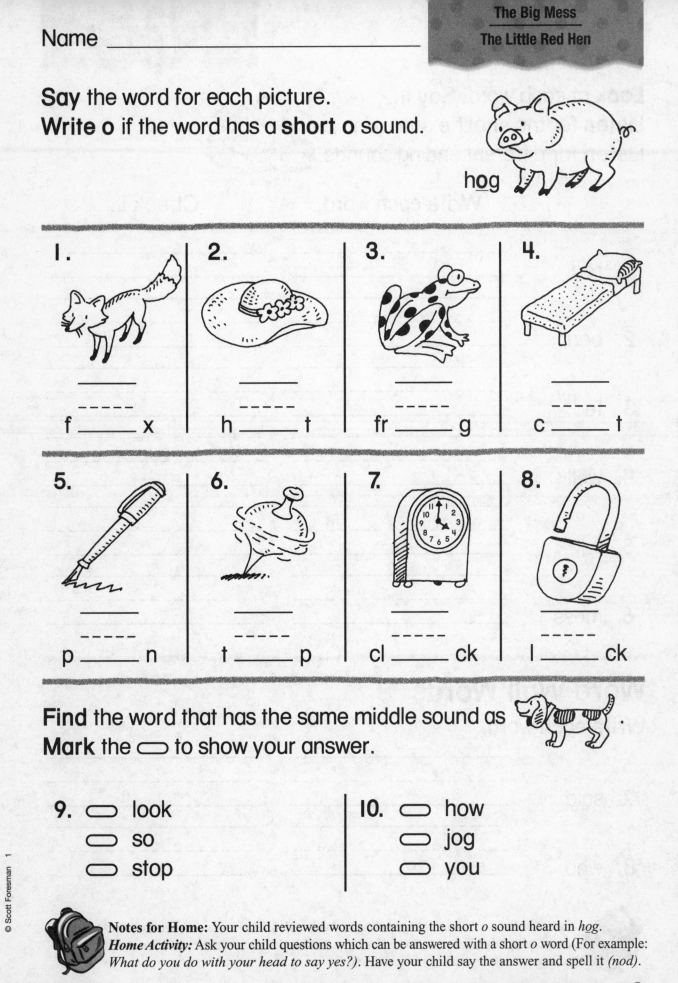

1.

f ___ x

2.

h ___ t

3.

fr ___ g

4.

c ___ t

5.

p ___ n

6.

t ___ p

7.

cl ___ ck

8.

l ___ ck

Find the word that has the same middle sound as [dog].
Mark the ⬭ to show your answer.

9. ⬭ look
⬭ so
⬭ stop

10. ⬭ how
⬭ jog
⬭ you

Notes for Home: Your child reviewed words containing the short *o* sound heard in *hog*.
Home Activity: Ask your child questions which can be answered with a short *o* word (For example: *What do you do with your head to say yes?*). Have your child say the answer and spell it *(nod)*.

Phonics: Short *o* Review **9**

Name _____

The Big Mess
The Little Red Hen

Look at each word. **Say** it.
Listen for the **short e** sound in
Listen for different ending sounds.

Write each word.   **Check** it.
_____   _____

1. red

2. bed

3. fed

4. well

5. tell

6. mess

Word Wall Words
Write each word.

7. said

8. who

Notes for Home: Your child spelled words with *-ed, -ell,* and *-ess* and two frequently used words: *said, who.* **Home Activity:** Have your child add other letters before *-ed, -ell,* and *-ess* to form new words, such as *led, bell,* and *Bess.*

10 Spelling: Word Families *-ed, -ell,* and *-ess*   Level 1.3

Name _____

Circle the noun that matches each picture.

many   little   fish

1. _____

hog   fat   sit

2. _____

hot   pans   three

3. _____

hen   eat   peck

4. _____

Write a noun to go with each picture.

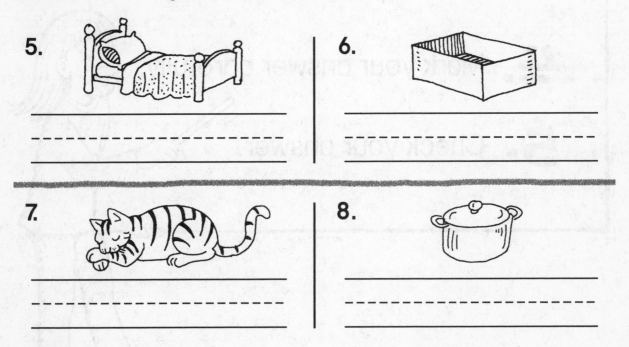

5. _____

6. _____

7. _____

8. _____

Notes for Home: Your child reviewed nouns—words that name people, places, animals, or things. **Home Activity:** Read a story book with your child and look for words that are nouns. Then ask your child to use those nouns in new sentences.

Test-Taking Tips

1. Write your name on the test.

2. Read each question twice.

3. Read all the answer choices for the question.

4. Mark your answer carefully.

5. Check your answer.

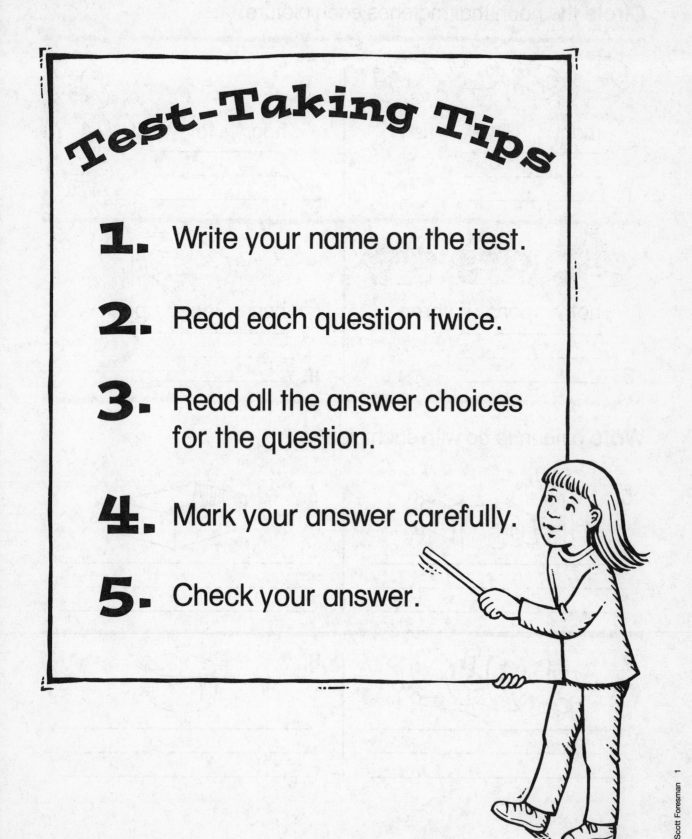

Name _____

Part 1: Vocabulary

Read each sentence.

Mark the ⬭ for the word that fits.

---

1. "I cannot do it," she _____ .
   - ⬭ saw
   - ⬭ now
   - ⬭ said

---

2. "_____ will help me?"
   - ⬭ Who
   - ⬭ On
   - ⬭ Why

---

3. Miko comes to _____ .
   - ⬭ into
   - ⬭ help
   - ⬭ went

---

4. _____ they walk up.
   - ⬭ So
   - ⬭ All
   - ⬭ Many

---

5. _____ they go down.
   - ⬭ Who
   - ⬭ By
   - ⬭ Now

GO ON ➡

© Scott Foresman 1

Part 2: Comprehension

Read each question.
Mark the ⬭ for the answer.

6. What does the Little Red Hen want?
   - ⬭ help
   - ⬭ pans
   - ⬭ a job

7. The dog, cat, and pig are not like the Little Red Hen.
   All they do is
   - ⬭ watch her work.
   - ⬭ sing a song.
   - ⬭ eat food.

8. Who makes the food?
   - ⬭ the Little Red Hen
   - ⬭ the cat
   - ⬭ the dog and the pig

9. At the end, the dog, cat, and pig are
   - ⬭ happy.
   - ⬭ sad.
   - ⬭ sick.

10. Was the Little Red Hen mean to eat by herself?
    - ⬭ Yes, because her friends helped.
    - ⬭ No, because she did all the work.
    - ⬭ Yes, because she made too much food.

Say the word for each picture.
Write -s if the picture shows more than one.

bat**s**

1. hen _____ _ _ _ _ _

2. pet _____ _ _ _ _ _

3. cat _____ _ _ _ _ _

4. web _____ _ _ _ _ _

5. dog _____ _ _ _ _ _

6. rat _____ _ _ _ _ _

7. pig _____ _ _ _ _ _

8. frog _____ _ _ _ _ _

Find the word that means more than one.
Mark the ⬭ to show your answer.

9. ⬭ boss
   ⬭ hats
   ⬭ his

10. ⬭ has
    ⬭ digs
    ⬭ pens

Notes for Home: Your child reviewed plural nouns that show more than one. *Home Activity:* Together, count and list objects in your home. Choose words that form their plurals by adding just an *-s.* Help your child spell the names of the objects, having him or her supply the *-s* ending.

Name _____

| red | bed | fed | well | tell | mess |

Write three words from the box that rhyme with **Ted**.

1. _____   2. _____   3. _____

Write two words from the box that rhyme with .

4. _____   5. _____

Write a word from the box to match each picture.

6. _____   7. _____   8. _____

Pick a word from the box to finish each sentence.
Write it on the line.

said
who

9. Oh, _____ will help me?

10. Is that what she _____ ?

Notes for Home: Your child spelled words that end with *-ed, -ell,* and *-ess* and two frequently-used words: *said, who.* **Home Activity:** Work with your child to make up fun rhymes using the spelling words. Help your child write the rhymes and draw pictures for the rhymes.

Family Times

Yes, We Want Some Too!

Cat Traps

Oh, Yes! They Do!

Blue jays like to peck and peck.
Oh, yes! They do!
Blackbirds eat fruit on the deck.
Oh, yes! They do!
I will watch them. Oh, yes! I will!
I will watch them. Oh, yes! I will!

Green frogs play next to a duck.
Oh, yes! They do!
Ten red hens say, "Cluck, cluck, cluck."
Oh, yes! They do!
I will watch them. Oh, yes! I will!
I will watch them. Oh, yes! I will!

This rhyme includes words your child is working with in school: words with the short *e* sound (*peck, yes*) and words with initial *r* and *l* blends (*blue*, *fruit*, *cluck*). Sing "Oh, Yes! They Do!" with your child. Then work together to draw the animals named in the rhyme.

(fold here)

Name: _____

You are your child's first and best teacher!

Here are ways to help your child practice skills while having fun!

Day 1 Write these blends on slips of paper: *dr, fr, tr; bl, cl, pl.* Invite your child to pick a slip and say a word that begins with that blend, such as *drop, frog,* or *trip.*

Day 2 At dinnertime, ask your child to use each of the following words in sentences about the food you will have: *for, good, some, too,* and *want.*

Day 3 Describe an everyday task without saying what the task is. Ask your child to guess the task. For example, to describe making a bed, say: *I pull up the sheet. I pull up the blanket,* and so on.

Day 4 After your child listens to a story or watches a favorite TV show, ask what happened in the story. Invite your child to write words and/or draw pictures that help retell the story.

Day 5 Take turns pointing to individual household objects, naming each object, and then telling the word that would mean more than one of that same object. For example, use *chair* and *chairs.*

Read with your child EVERY DAY!

Follow the Path

Materials 15 index cards, marker, 1 button per player

Game Directions

1. Write the 15 letters shown below on index cards.

2. Shuffle the cards and place them facedown in a pile.

3. Players take turns picking a card from the pile and writing as many short *e* words as possible beginning with the letter on the card.

4. Each player moves his or her button forward for every word named.

5. The first player to reach the end wins!

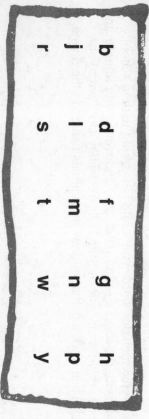

b	d	f	g	h
j	l	m	n	p
r	s	t	w	y

2

3

Name _____

Circle the word for each picture.

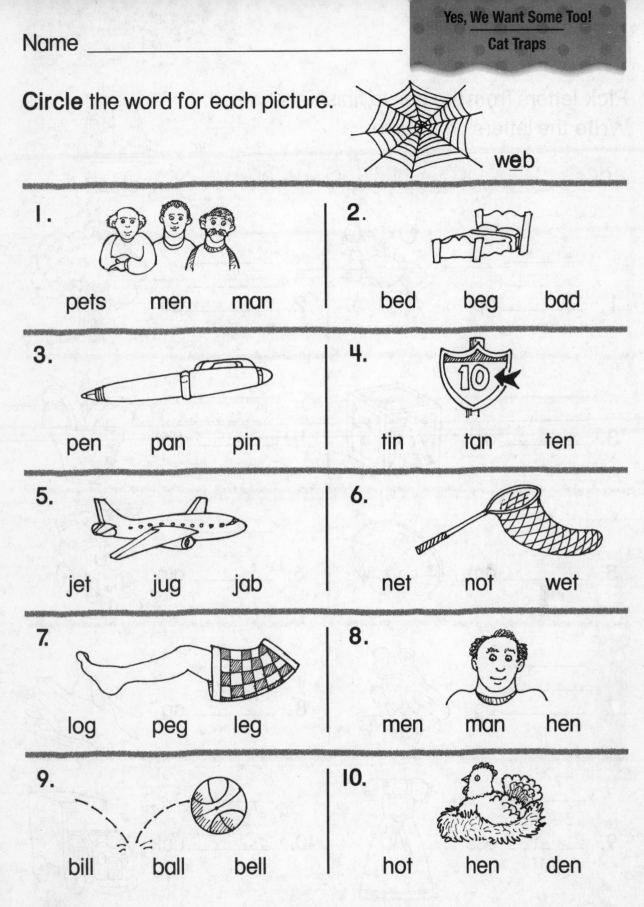

w<u>e</u>b

1.

pets   men   man

2.

bed   beg   bad

3.

pen   pan   pin

4.

tin   tan   ten

5.

jet   jug   jab

6.

net   not   wet

7.

log   peg   leg

8.

men   man   hen

9.

bill   ball   bell

10.

hot   hen   den

Notes for Home: Your child practiced reading words with the short *e* sound (l<u>e</u>g, w<u>e</u>b).
Home Activity: Help your child write a short story using the short *e* words on this page.

Level 1.3   **Phonics: Short *e***   **19**

Pick letters from the box to finish each word.
Write the letters on the line.

clock

| dr | fr | tr | bl | cl | pl |

1. _____ op

2. _____ ee

3. _____ ock

4. _____ ant

5. _____ am

6. _____ ain

7. _____ og

8. _____ ap

9. _____ ess

10. _____ uck

Notes for Home: Your child is learning to read words with initial *r* and *l* blends (*trap*, *frog*, *clam*).
Home Activity: Ask your child to make up silly sentences that each contain words beginning with just one blend, such as *Freddy frog likes French fries.*

Pick a word from the box to finish each sentence.
Write it on the line. Use each word only once.

for	good	some	too	want

1. Do you _____ to eat?

2. Yes, I want _____ food.

3. Here is some food _____ you.

4. That looks _____ .

5. I will eat some _____ .

Notes for Home: This week your child is learning to read the words *for*, *good, some, too,* and *want*. **Home Activity:** Get puppets or use washable markers to draw a face on closed fingers for puppets. Use the puppets to have a dialogue with your child using these new words.

Look at each picture.
Make an X after the sentence that tells what happened.

1. Tom got a cat. _____
   Tom fell in the water. _____

2. Ming likes pets. _____
   Ming likes fish. _____

3. Tess likes to sing. _____
   Tess ran up the big hill. _____

4. The cat wants the fish. _____
   The fish like the cat. _____

Look at the picture.
Write a word to finish the sentence.

5. The girl is _____ .

Notes for Home: Your child is learning about drawing conclusions about story events and characters. **Home Activity:** Draw faces that show simple emotions: sadness, joy, anger, and so on. Ask your child to tell you how each person you drew feels, and explain how he or she knew this.

Name _____

Adding an **-s** can make a noun mean more than one.

Cat shows one.
Cats show more than one.   **cat**   **cats**

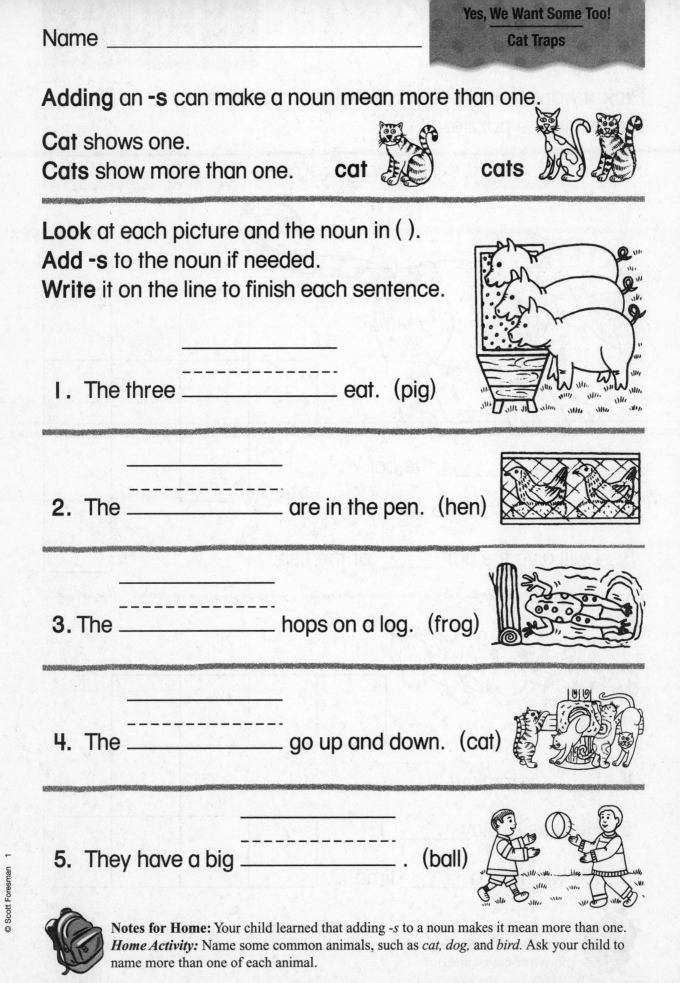

Look at each picture and the noun in ( ).
Add -s to the noun if needed.
Write it on the line to finish each sentence.

1. The three _____ eat. (pig)

---

2. The _____ are in the pen. (hen)

---

3. The _____ hops on a log. (frog)

---

4. The _____ go up and down. (cat)

---

5. They have a big _____ . (ball)

Notes for Home: Your child learned that adding -s to a noun makes it mean more than one.
Home Activity: Name some common animals, such as *cat, dog,* and *bird.* Ask your child to name more than one of each animal.

© Scott Foresman 1

Pick a word from the box to finish each sentence.
Write it in the puzzle.

| for | good | meow | some | too | want |

1. The fish is _____ the cat.

2. "_____ !" said the cat.

3. I will give the cat _____ of the fish.

4. I _____ to play!

5. He likes to play _____ !

6. We will have a _____ time.

 Notes for Home: Your child solved puzzles using the words *for, good, meow, some, too,* and *want.* **Home Activity:** Say each word and ask your child to use it in a sentence. Help your child write each sentence.

Name _____

Say the word for each picture.
Write o if the word has a **short o** sound.

l<u>o</u>g

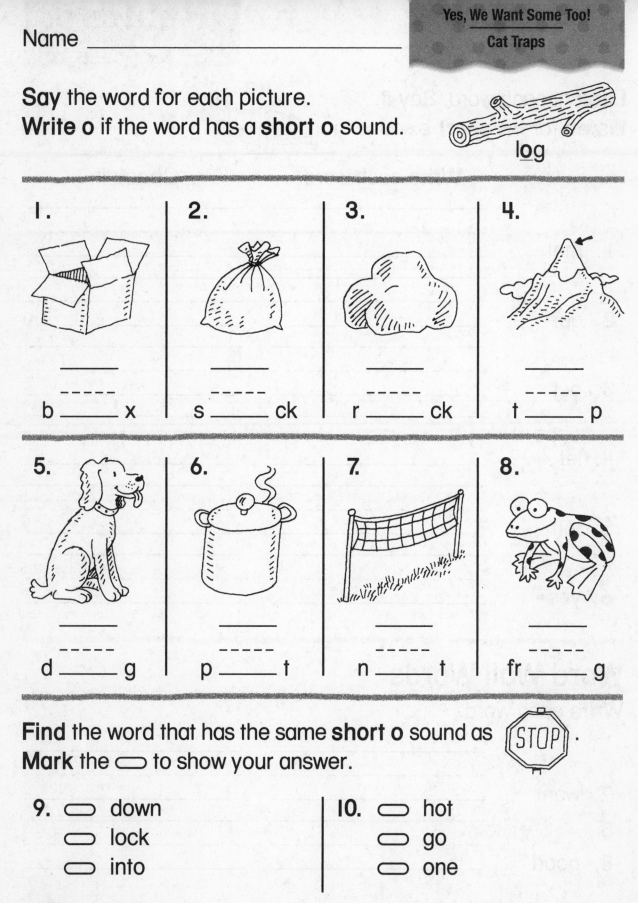

1.

b _____ x

2.

s _____ ck

3.

r _____ ck

4.

t _____ p

5.

d _____ g

6.

p _____ t

7.

n _____ t

8.

fr _____ g

Find the word that has the same **short o** sound as STOP.
Mark the ⬭ to show your answer.

9. ⬭ down
   ⬭ lock
   ⬭ into

10. ⬭ hot
    ⬭ go
    ⬭ one

Notes for Home: Your child reviewed words with the short _o_ sound heard in _log_.
Home Activity: Have your child look through a book and find short _o_ words. Together, list
these words. Take turns using these words in sentences.

Name _____

Look at each word. **Say** it.
Listen for the **short e** sound in

Write each word.   **Check** it.

1. met

2. get

3. pet

4. let

5. ten

6. yes

Word Wall Words

Write each word.

7. want

8. good

Notes for Home: Your child spelled words with the short *e* sound heard in *bed* and two
frequently used words: *want, good.* **Home Activity:** Encourage your child to use some of these
words to write a story about a pet that takes a walk on a rainy day.

Say the word for each picture.
Write the plural for each word.

1. dog

_____
- - - - - - - - - -

2. sock

_____
- - - - - - - - - -

3. hen

_____
- - - - - - - - - -

4. bell

_____
- - - - - - - - - -

5. flag

_____
- - - - - - - - - -

6. pet

_____
- - - - - - - - - -

7. fish

_____
- - - - - - - - - -

8. man

_____
- - - - - - - - - -

9. map

_____
- - - - - - - - - -

Notes for Home: Your child reviewed nouns that become plural when just -*s* is added and irregular plurals like *men* and *fish*. **Home Activity:** Look at a picture book with your child. List several nouns. Include both singular and plural nouns.

Name _____

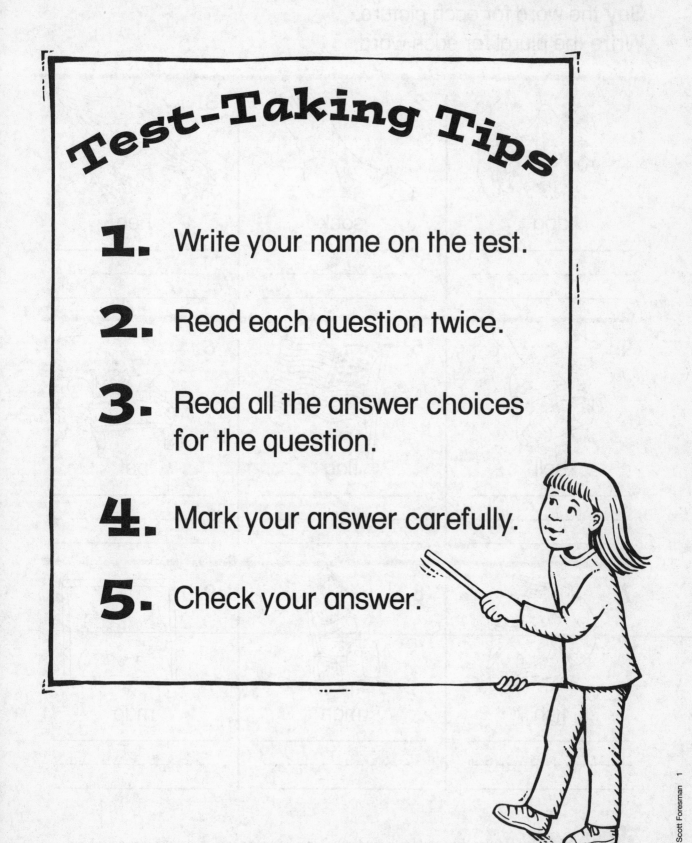

Test-Taking Tips

1. Write your name on the test.

2. Read each question twice.

3. Read all the answer choices for the question.

4. Mark your answer carefully.

5. Check your answer.

© Scott Foresman 1

Part I: Vocabulary

Read each sentence.
Mark the ⬭ for the word that fits.

I. The cats _____ to eat.
⬭ make   ⬭ want   ⬭ sing

---

2. The cats get _____ chow.
⬭ on   ⬭ some   ⬭ into

---

3. Now they meow _____ more.
⬭ how   ⬭ away   ⬭ for

---

4. The chow was _____ .
⬭ good   ⬭ them   ⬭ happy

---

5. This cat is _____ fat!
⬭ all   ⬭ by   ⬭ too

GO ON ➡

Part 2: Comprehension

Read each question.
Mark the ⬭ for the answer.

6. In this story, the cat wants to
   - ⬭ nap.
   - ⬭ snack.
   - ⬭ fish.

7. What does the cat do many times?
   - ⬭ sets a trap
   - ⬭ gets a bug
   - ⬭ eats a snack

8. The cat gets a snack from a
   - ⬭ pig.
   - ⬭ duck.
   - ⬭ girl.

9. How does the cat feel at the end?
   - ⬭ mad
   - ⬭ sick
   - ⬭ happy

10. What can you tell about the cat?
    - ⬭ He runs fast.
    - ⬭ He has bad luck.
    - ⬭ He eats too much.

Use the word in ( ) to finish each sentence.
Write it on the line.
Add an **-s** if needed.

The cat **smells** a rat.
The rats **get** away.

_____
(see)
- - - - - - - - - - -
1. The cat _____ a fish.

_____
(look)
- - - - - - - - - - -
2. The two fish _____ at him.

_____
(hit)
- - - - - - - - - - -
3. The cat _____ the fish.

_____
(get)
- - - - - - - - - - -
4. The cat _____ wet!

Find the sentence that tells about the picture.
Mark the ⬭ to show your answer.

5. ⬭ The rat win.
   ⬭ The rats wins.
   ⬭ The rat wins.

Notes for Home: Your child reviewed verbs that end in -s that describe what just one person or thing does. **Home Activity:** With your child, watch television with the sound off. Have your child tell what is happening, using the appropriate verbs.

| met | get | pet | let | ten | yes |

Change one letter in each word to make a word from the box.
Write the new word on the line.

1. got _____

2. leg _____

3. pen _____

4. men _____

5. tin _____

6. yet _____

Pick a word from the box to match each clue.
Write it on the line.

7. not no _____

8. 5 + 5 = _____

Pick a word from the box to finish each sentence.
Write it on the line.

| want | good |

9. I _____ a hen.

10. A hen is a _____ pet.

Notes for Home: Your child spelled words with the short *e* sound heard in *get* and two frequently used words: *want, good*. **Home Activity:** Write the spelling words. Cut each word into letters. Have your child use the letters to spell each word.

Family Times

Biscuit

My Buddy, Stan

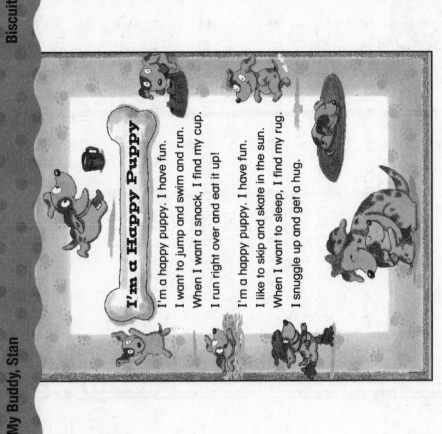

I'm a Happy Puppy

I'm a happy puppy. I have fun.
I want to jump and swim and run.
When I want a snack, I find my cup.
I run right over and eat it up!

I'm a happy puppy. I have fun.
I like to skip and skate in the sun.
When I want to sleep, I find my rug.
I snuggle up and get a hug.

This rhyme includes words that your child is working with in school: words with the short *u* vowel sound (*fun, cup*) and words that begin with the letter *s* and another consonant (*skip, snack*). Sing "I'm a Happy Puppy" with your child. Make up hand motions to match the words in the rhyme.

(fold here)

Name: _____

You are your child's first and best teacher!

Here are ways to help your child practice skills while having fun!

Day 1 Write a simple short *u* word, such as *hug*. Have your child change one letter to make a new word with short *u*, such as *bug*. Take turns changing that word to *bun* and *sun* and so on.

Day 2 Encourage your child to make up sentences that include the following words: *jump, more, sleep, time,* and *with.* Then ask your child to draw a picture that illustrates each sentence.

Day 3 Your child is learning to identify the main idea in a story. Read a story aloud to your child. Then ask your child: *What is the story all about?*

Day 4 Your child is learning about grouping things that belong together. Give your child a category such as *pets* or *fruit.* Have your child name things that belong in that category.

Day 5 Work with your child to make an address book filled with friends and family. Make sure that your child capitalizes all special names and places (proper nouns).

Read with your child EVERY DAY!

S Is the Best

Materials paper circle, paper clip, pencils, 1 button per player

Game Directions

1. Make a simple spinner as shown.

2. Take turns spinning and naming a word that begins with the s blend spun.

3. If the player names a word, he or she may move that number of spaces. If the player cannot name a word, the turn is over.

4. The first player to reach the end wins!

sc	sk
3	2
st	sn
1	3
sp	sw
2	4
sl	sm
4	1

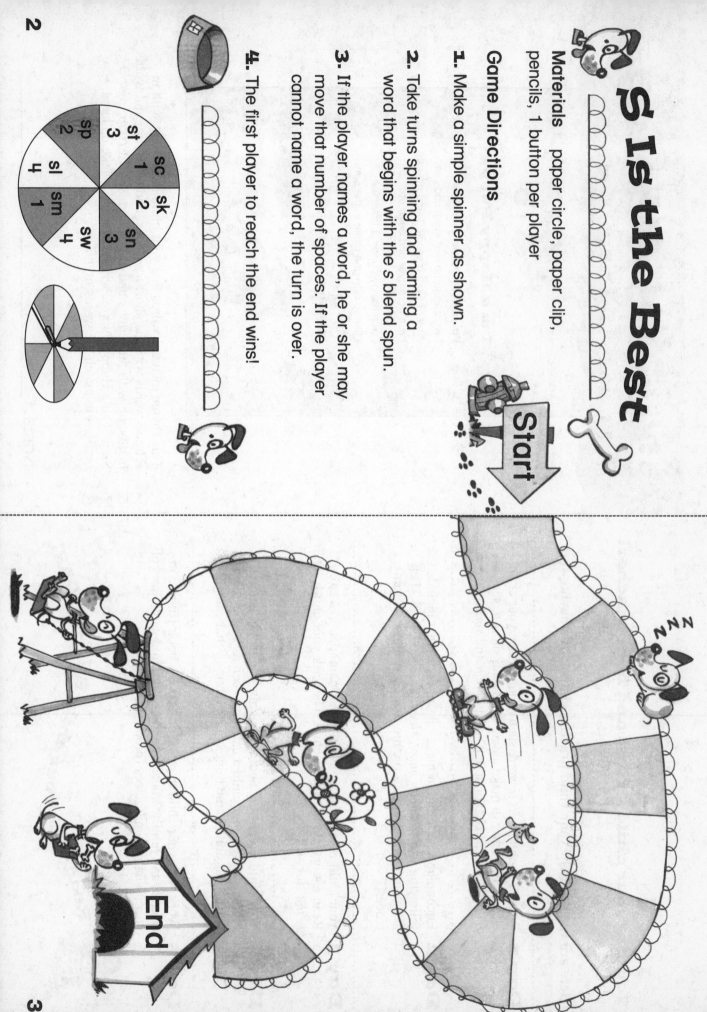

Start

End

Name _____

Circle a word to finish each sentence.
Write it on the line.

p<u>u</u>p

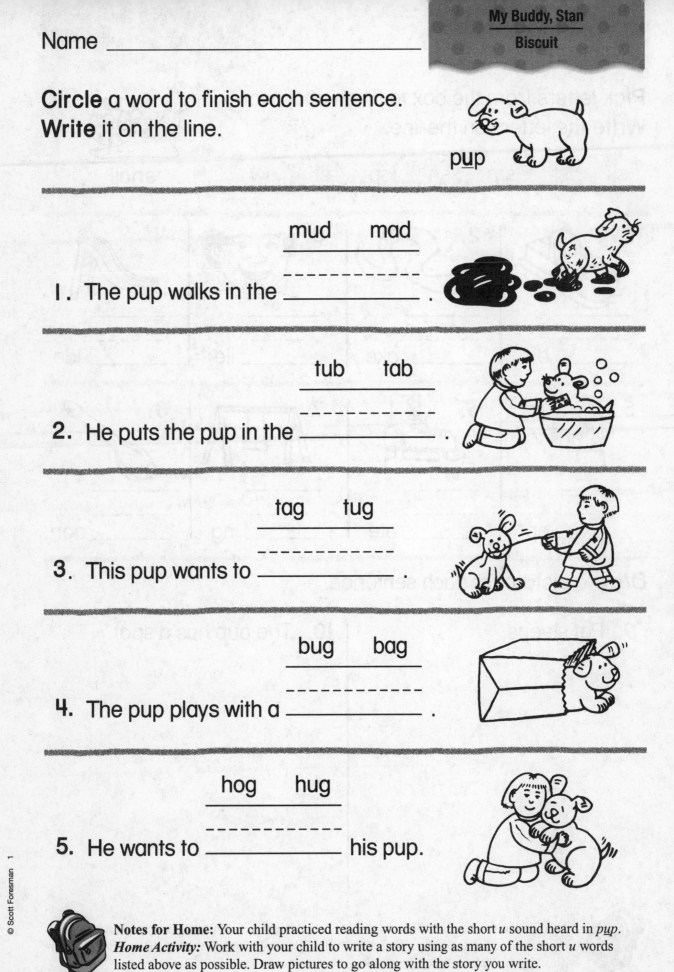

mud   mad

- - - - - - - - - - -

1. The pup walks in the _____ .

tub   tab

- - - - - - - - - - -

2. He puts the pup in the _____ .

tag   tug

- - - - - - - - - - -

3. This pup wants to _____ .

bug   bag

- - - - - - - - - - -

4. The pup plays with a _____ .

hog   hug

- - - - - - - - - - -

5. He wants to _____ his pup.

Notes for Home: Your child practiced reading words with the short *u* sound heard in *pup*.
Home Activity: Work with your child to write a story using as many of the short *u* words
listed above as possible. Draw pictures to go along with the story you write.

Pick letters from the box to finish each word.
Write the letters on the line.

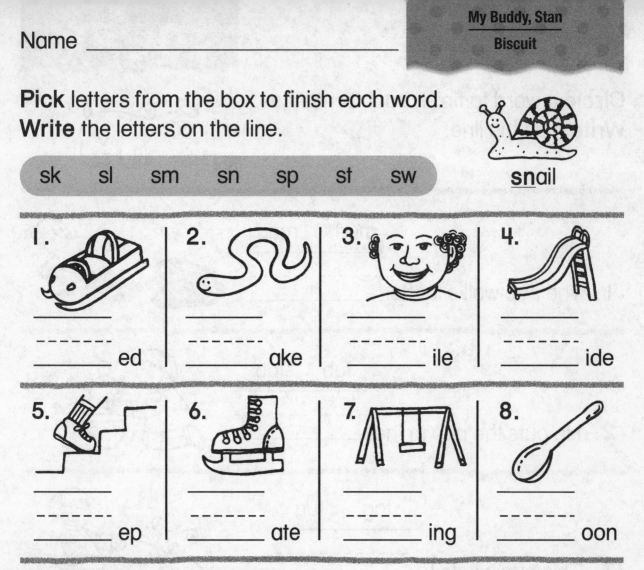

| sk | sl | sm | sn | sp | st | sw |

snail

1. _____ ed

2. _____ ake

3. _____ ile

4. _____ ide

5. _____ ep

6. _____ ate

7. _____ ing

8. _____ oon

Draw a picture for each sentence.

9. Pat sleeps.

10. The pup has a spot.

Notes for Home: Your child identified words that begin with *s* blends such as *sp* and *sn* (*spool*, *snail*). **Home Activity:** Work with your child to find things around the house that begin with *s* blends. Make a list of these items.

Pick a word from the box to finish each sentence.
Write it on the line. Use each word only once.

| jump | more | sleep | time | with |

1. It is _____ for bed.

2. Tim wants to _____ .

3. The pup wants to _____ .

4. The pup gets one _____ hug.

5. The pup will sleep _____ Tim.

Notes for Home: This week your child is learning to read the words *jump, more, sleep, time,*
and *with*. **Home Activity:** Together with your child, write a short poem about a new puppy.
Use as many of the words on this page as possible.

Name _____

Read the story.

Circle the sentence that tells what the story is all about.

Draw a picture that shows what the story is all about.

1. Nan got a pup.   2.
   The pup is black.
   Nan hugs the pup.
   Nan calls the pup Bud.

3. Ted jumps into the water.   4.
   Dan runs into the water.
   Ted swims with Dan.
   Ted and Dan have fun.

Write the name of a story you have read.

Draw a picture that shows what the story is all about.

5. _____

Notes for Home: Your child identified the main idea of a story. *Home Activity:* Read a story to your child. Discuss the story and ask your child to tell you what the story is all about. Invite your child to draw a picture that shows what the story is all about.

Special names for people, places, animals, and things begin with **capital letters.**

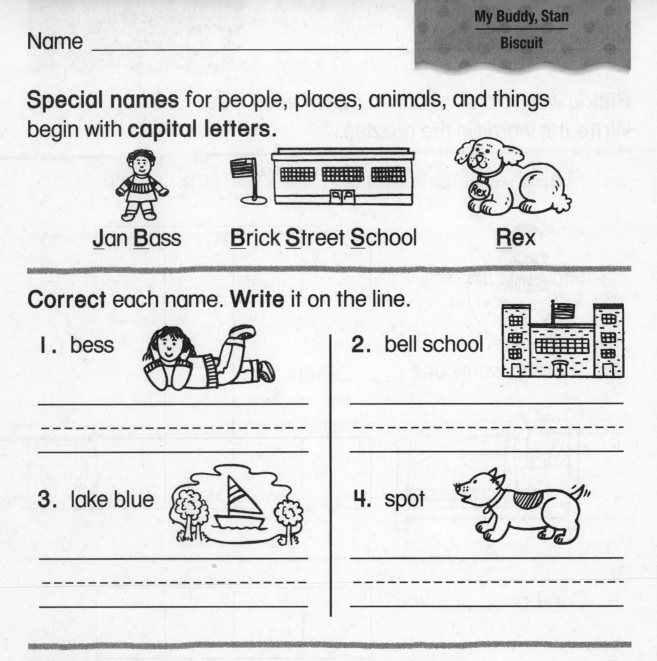

Jan Bass   Brick Street School   Rex

Correct each name. **Write** it on the line.

1. bess

2. bell school

3. lake blue

4. spot

Draw a special person, place, thing, or animal.
Write its name on the line.

5.

_____

Notes for Home: Your child identified and wrote special names (proper nouns) with capital letters. *Home Activity:* Work with your child to think of the names of favorite people, places, or pets. Help your child to write a list of these names using capital letters.

Pick a word from the box to match each clue.
Write the words in the puzzles.

| hear | jump | more | sleep | time | with |

1.

2. The pup wants one _____ hug.

3.

4. Can I go _____ you?

5. It is _____ for bed.

6.

Notes for Home: Your child completed puzzles using words that he or she learned to read this week. **Home Activity:** Work with your child to write sentences using these words. Have him or her read the sentences aloud to you.

© Scott Foresman 1

Name _____

Circle the word for each picture.
Write it on the line.

v<u>e</u>t

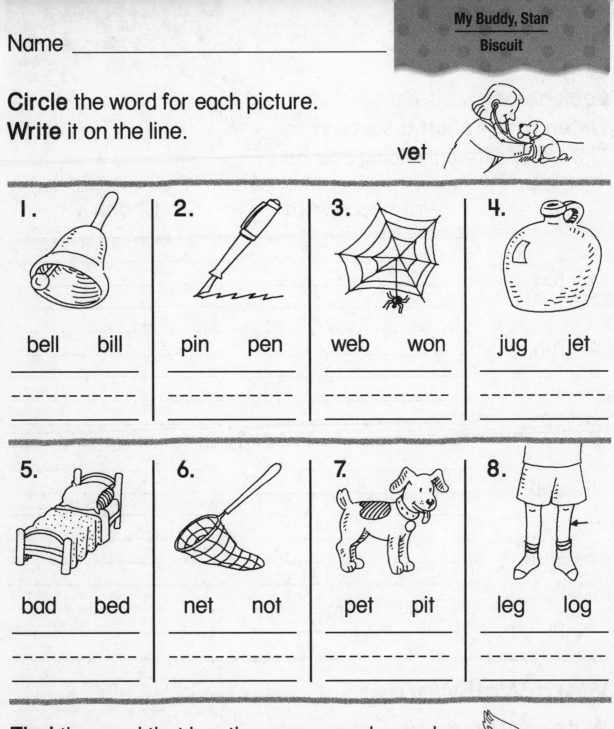

1.
bell   bill

2.
pin   pen

3.
web   won

4.
jug   jet

5.
bad   bed

6.
net   not

7.
pet   pit

8.
leg   log

Find the word that has the same vowel sound as .
Mark the ⬭ to show your answer.

9. ⬭ sleep
⬭ sled
⬭ slap

10. ⬭ well
⬭ wall
⬭ we

Notes for Home: Your child reviewed words with the short *e* sound heard in *vet*. **Home Activity:** Help your child write a silly poem in which all the rhyming words have the short *e* sound. Encourage your child to read the poem aloud to other family members.

Look at each word. **Say** it.
Listen for the **short u** sound in .
Listen for different ending sounds.

	Write each word.	**Check** it.
1. fun		
2. run		
3. up		
4. cup		
5. stuff		
6. puff		

Word Wall Words

Write each word.

7. jump		
8. more		

Notes for Home: Your child spelled words with *-un, -up,* and *-uff* that have the short *u* sound heard in *cup* and two frequently used words: *jump, more.* **Home Activity:** Say each spelling word. Have your child use it in a sentence. Say the spelling word again and have your child write it.

© Scott Foresman 1

Circle the special name in each sentence.

1. I call my dog Max.

2. Here is Meg.

3. Her cat, Sam, is big and fat.

4. That little cat is Pip.

5. Dan Yin has a pig.

Circle the special name in each sentence.
Write it with a capital letter on the line.

6. Where is bess? _____

7. She is with fran. _____

8. How many rats does kim have? _____

9. Let brad hold my frog. _____

10. Where did nan get all the bugs? _____

Notes for Home: Your child identified and wrote proper nouns—names for particular people, places, or things. *Home Activity:* Have your child write some address labels for your mail, making sure the proper names are capitalized.

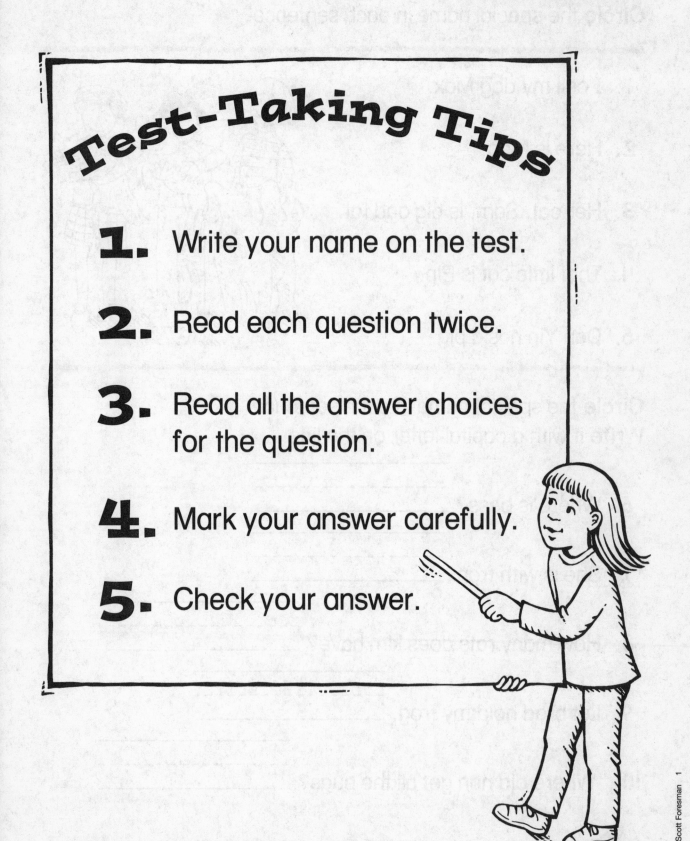

Test-Taking Tips

1. Write your name on the test.

2. Read each question twice.

3. Read all the answer choices for the question.

4. Mark your answer carefully.

5. Check your answer.

Part 1: Vocabulary

Read each sentence.
Mark the ⬭ for the word that fits.

1. The pup likes to _____ .
   ⬭ more   ⬭ make   ⬭ jump

2. The pup plays _____ the girl.
   ⬭ with   ⬭ this   ⬭ some

3. The pup gets one _____ snack.
   ⬭ help   ⬭ more   ⬭ now

4. It is _____ for bed.
   ⬭ time   ⬭ jump   ⬭ sleep

5. The pup will _____ now.
   ⬭ some   ⬭ sleep   ⬭ time

GO ON ➡

Part 2: Comprehension

Read each question.

Mark the ⬭ for the answer.

6. What is it time for Biscuit to do?
   - ⬭ play
   - ⬭ eat
   - ⬭ sleep

7. Biscuit does not go to bed. Biscuit wants to
   - ⬭ eat.
   - ⬭ hear a story.
   - ⬭ kiss a doll.

8. How is Biscuit like a baby?
   - ⬭ He can say "Woof."
   - ⬭ He can sing.
   - ⬭ He likes hugs.

9. How does the story end?
   - ⬭ The girl plays.
   - ⬭ Biscuit sleeps.
   - ⬭ Biscuit runs away.

10. What is a good name for this story?
    - ⬭ "A Happy Girl"
    - ⬭ "Time for Bed"
    - ⬭ "One More Walk"

© Scott Foresman 1

Name _____

Circle the word for each picture.
Write it on the line.

do**ll**

1.

puff   pull

_____

2.

snip   sniff

_____

3.

stuns   stuff

_____

4.

miss   mitt

_____

5.

kiss   kick

_____

6.

bat   ball

_____

7.

tops   toss

_____

8.

buzz   bull

_____

Find the word that has the same ending sound as .
Mark the ⬭ to show your answer.

9. ⬭ vet
⬭ still
⬭ walk

10. ⬭ smell
⬭ black
⬭ yellow

Notes for Home: Your child reviewed words that have double final consonants such as *doll*.
Home Activity: Have your child collect words like these from signs and stories and then write
the found words in lists. Invite him or her to keep a separate list for each letter pair.

Level 1.3   **Phonics: Double Final Consonants Review** **47**

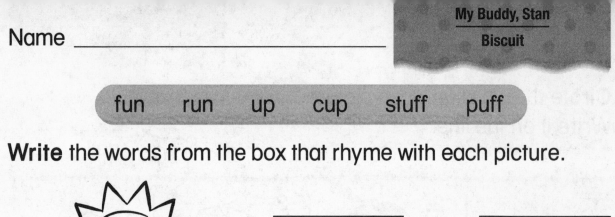

fun   run   up   cup   stuff   puff

Write the words from the box that rhyme with each picture.

1. _____   2. _____

3. _____   4. _____

5. _____   6. _____

Pick a word from the box to finish each sentence.
Write it on the line.

jump   more

7. My pup likes to _____ up.

8. He wants one _____ hug.

Notes for Home: Your child spelled words with *-un, -up,* and *-uff* that have the short *u* sound heard in *cup* and two frequently used words: *jump, more.* **Home Activity:** Help your child make up rhymes using some of these spelling words.

Family Times

Trucks

Communities

Trucks and Buses

Cindy's a plumber.
She unclogs a tub.
She unclogs a sink too
And gives it a scrub!

George drives a big truck,
With his puppy in back.
George has all the lumber
In one giant stack.

Gene is a driver.
He drives a big bus.
Gene drives in the city
And drives all of us.

This rhyme includes words your child is working with in school: words with the short *u* sound (*tub, truck*) and words beginning with *g* and *c* that stand for the sounds /j/ and /s/ (*Gene, city*). Sing "Trucks and Buses" with your child. Then draw and label pictures of trucks and buses.

(fold here)

Name: _____

You are your child's first and best teacher!

Here are ways to help your child practice skills while having fun!

Day 1 With your child, practice saying these words that begin with the sound /s/: *cell, cellar, cement, cent, center, circle, circus, city,* and *cycle.* Hiss like a snake when you say the sound /s/.

Day 2 Make up two-line rhymes with your child, using each of these words: *bring, carry, hold, our,* and *us.* For example: *I love to carry/My big pig, Harry.*

Day 3 Write the phrase *Have Four Legs.* With your child, take turns thinking of things that have four legs, including animals and furniture.

Day 4 Your child is learning to make announcements. Give your child the job of announcing your dinner menu.

Day 5 Practice using special titles. Have fun with your child by using *Ms., Mrs., Mr.,* and *Dr.* before the names of your pets and other animals you both know.

Read with your child EVERY DAY!

It's a Match

Materials paper, marker, bag

Game Directions

1. Write the short *u* words shown below on small squares of paper. Place the squares in a bag.

2. Players take turns picking squares from the bag, reading the words aloud, and placing each word over the picture it matches.

3. Play until the gameboard squares are all covered.

4. Make your own gameboard and set of matching short *u* words and play again.

Matching Words
bug, cup, duck, bus, tub, drum, skunk, truck

Name _____

Circle a word to finish each sentence.
Write it on the line.

d<u>u</u>ck

---

bun   bat   bus

_____

- - - - - - - - - -

1. Here is the _____ .

---

hug   tug   tag

_____

- - - - - - - - - -

2. Rob sees the ducks _____ .

---

run   ran   rip

_____

- - - - - - - - - -

3. Rob sees the ducks _____ .

---

mad   mud   bud

_____

- - - - - - - - - -

4. One duck fell in the _____ .

---

fan   fin   fun

_____

- - - - - - - - - -

5. Now the ducks have _____ !

Notes for Home: Your child practiced reading and writing words with the short *u* sound heard in *bug* and *duck*. **Home Activity:** Work together to write a poem using as many of the short *u* words shown above as you can.

Name _____

Say the word for each picture.
Circle the letter that begins each word.
Write the letter on the line.

circus   giraffe

g c
1. _____ ym

g c
2. _____ ent

g c
3. _____ ircle

g c
4. _____ ingerbread

g c
5. _____ erbil

g c
6. _____ erms

g c
7. _____ ity

g c
8. _____ ereal

Notes for Home: Your child practiced writing words that begin with *c* and *g* that stand for the /s/ sound in *circus* and the /j/ sound in *giraffe*. **Home Activity:** Ask your child to say the *c* /s/ and *g* /j/ words on this page out loud, emphasizing the initial sounds.

52 Phonics: Initial *c* /s/ and *g* /j/   Level 1.3

Pick a word from the box to finish each sentence.
Write it on the line.

bring   carry   hold   our   us

1. Dad, what did you _____ us?

2. Dad got _____ a truck!

3. _____ cat likes the truck.

4. The truck can _____ the cat to bed.

5. The truck can _____ one cat.

Notes for Home: This week your child is learning to read the words *bring, carry, hold, our,* and *us.* **Home Activity:** Work with your child to write three sentences using all five words.

Look at the pictures. Read the sentence.
Circle the word in ( ) that tells how the objects are alike.

fish   cat   pup

1. A fish, a cat, and a pup are all (pets, red).

cup   tub   glass

2. A cup, a tub, and a glass all hold (frogs, water).

bus   truck   van

3. You (skip, go) in a bus, a truck, and a van.

bat   ball   block

4. You (play, sing) with a bat, a ball, and a block.

ham   plum   nut

5. You (eat, walk) a ham, a plum, and a nut.

Notes for Home: Your child is learning about classifying—grouping things belonging together.
Home Activity: Draw three smiling faces and one sad one. Ask your child which one does not
belong and why.

A **title** comes before a name.
A title and a name each begin with
a capital letter.
A title ends with a ▪ .

Dr. Ron

Write each title and name on the line.
Use capital letters and a period.

1. One man in the bus is mr hob.

    _____

    - - - - - - - - - - - - - - - - - -

    _____

2. He brings ms woo to our class.

    _____

    - - - - - - - - - - - - - - - - - -

    _____

3. He brings mrs dan to the city.

    _____

    - - - - - - - - - - - - - - - - - -

    _____

4. We carry our pup, mr jump, on the bus.

    _____

    - - - - - - - - - - - - - - - - - -

    _____

---

5. dr ron can help our pup.

    _____

    - - - - - - - - - - - - - - - - - -

    _____

Notes for Home: Your child identified and wrote special titles, such as *Dr., Mr., Mrs.,* and *Ms.*
Home Activity: Put titles before the names of family friends. Say the names out loud. Help
your child write each title and name.

Pick the word from the box to finish each sentence.
Write it on the line. Use each word only once.

| bring | build | carry | hold | our | us |

1. Look at _____ go.

2. We are in _____ van.

3. Dad will _____ us to the water.

4. We _____ a cup, a ball, and a truck.

5. The cup can _____ water.

6. We play and _____ a city.

Notes for Home: Your child used newly learned words to fill in the blanks in a story.
Home Activity: Say each vocabulary word aloud, and have your child write it down.

Name _____

Write the words in each box in **ABC order**.

a b c d e f g h i j k l m n o p q r s t u v w x y z

help work fix save	truck dump rocks logs

1. _____

2. _____

3. _____

4. _____

5. _____

6. _____

7. _____

8. _____

Find these words in Words to Know of your student book on page 130. **Draw** a picture to show what these words mean.

9. dentist

10. coach

Notes for Home: Your child put words in alphabetical order and used a glossary to find the meanings of two words. *Home Activity:* Write the names of family members on slips of paper. Each name should begin with a different letter. Ask your child to put them in ABC order.

Name _____

Say the word for each picture.
Add -s to the word if it names more than one.

spot**s**

1. _____ _____
truck _____

2. _____ _____
slug _____

3. _____ _____
mat _____

4. _____ _____
doll _____

5. _____ _____
plum _____

6. _____ _____
egg _____

7. _____ _____
jug _____

8. _____ _____
mitt _____

Find the words that tell about the picture.
Mark the ⬭ to show your answer.

9. ⬭ three frog
   ⬭ three frogs
   ⬭ frog

10. ⬭ rock
    ⬭ two rock
    ⬭ two rocks

Notes for Home: Your child reviewed writing plural nouns by adding -s. **Home Activity:** Go through a grocery flyer with your child. Look for fruits and vegetables that form their plurals by adding only -s. Have your child use the plural forms to make a pretend shopping list.

Look at each word. **Say** it.
Listen for the **short u** sound in

Write each word.   **Check** it.

1. us

2. bus

3. cut

4. but

5. rug

6. hug

Word Wall Words

Write each word.

7. our

8. bring

Notes for Home: Your child spelled words with the short *u* sound heard in c*u*p and two frequently used words: *our, bring.* **Home Activity:** Have your child cut out letters for these spelling words from an old magazine and then paste the letters on paper to spell the words.

Read each name.
Write it correctly on the line.
Use a capital letter or a · if needed.

1. mr Lee _____

2. mrs Bell _____

3. miss fox _____

4. dr Dunn _____

Make a name tag for yourself.

Hello

5. I'm _____

Notes for Home: Your child reviewed writing special titles used with people's names.
Home Activity: Have your child help you make a phone list of the people to be called in emergencies. Say the names for your child to write. Use titles, such as *Dr.* or *Mrs.*

Part I: Vocabulary

Read each sentence.

Mark the ⊂⊃ for the word that fits.

1. This is _____ mom.
   - ⊂⊃ and
   - ⊂⊃ our
   - ⊂⊃ many

2. Mom will go with _____ .
   - ⊂⊃ all
   - ⊂⊃ by
   - ⊂⊃ us

3. She can _____ the bag.
   - ⊂⊃ stop
   - ⊂⊃ carry
   - ⊂⊃ come

4. I will _____ the door.
   - ⊂⊃ play
   - ⊂⊃ make
   - ⊂⊃ hold

5. Sal will _____ a bag in for Mom.
   - ⊂⊃ bring
   - ⊂⊃ sing
   - ⊂⊃ find

GO ON

Part 2: Comprehension

Read each question.

Mark the ⬭ for the answer.

6. Who helps us stay healthy?
   - ⬭ doctors
   - ⬭ police officers
   - ⬭ coaches

7. Teachers help us to
   - ⬭ sleep.
   - ⬭ learn.
   - ⬭ build.

8. Who can fix our teeth?
   - ⬭ mail carriers
   - ⬭ dentists
   - ⬭ firefighters

9. What did you learn from what you read?
   - ⬭ Mail carriers have the best job.
   - ⬭ There are many kinds of work.
   - ⬭ Kids can have jobs.

10. What is a good name for what you read?
    - ⬭ "Go to the Doctor"
    - ⬭ "Time to Play"
    - ⬭ "Jobs People Do"

Pick letters from the box to finish each word.
Write the letters on the line.

truck

| br | cr | dr | fr | gr | pr |

1.

_____
_____ ick

2.

_____
_____ og

3.

_____
_____ um

4.

_____
_____ op

5.

_____
_____ack

6.

_____
_____ in

7.

_____
_____ ess

8.

_____
_____ ib

Find the word that has the same beginning sound as [train].
Mark the ⬭ to show your answer.

9. ⬭ trip
   ⬭ drill
   ⬭ brim

10. ⬭ grab
    ⬭ trot
    ⬭ tan

Notes for Home: Your child reviewed words that begin with the letters *br, cr, dr, fr, gr, pr,* and *tr.* **Home Activity:** Read a story with your child. Look for words that begin with these letters. Encourage your child to read these words.

| us | bus | cut | but | rug | hug |

Write the words from the box that rhyme with **hut**.

1. _____

2. _____

Write the words from the box that rhyme with **Gus**.

3. _____

4. _____

Write the words from the box that rhyme with **dug**.

5. _____

6. _____

Pick a word from the box to finish each sentence.
Write it in the puzzle.

7. I have my hat.
   We have _____ hats.

8. _____ it to me.

| our | bring |

Notes for Home: Your child practiced spelling words with the short *u* sound in *pup* and two frequently used words: *our, bring.* **Home Activity:** Use these spelling words to make up letter games with your child. (For example: *Change* <u>rat</u> *to* <u>but</u> *in two turns.* rat bat but.)

Family Times

Fox and Bear

Fox and Bear Look at the Moon

My Pals

My pals help when I am ill.
My best pals are Pam and Jill.
Pam will fix a yummy lunch.
She will fix me toast to munch.
Jill will hand me my red cup.
It has milk. I drink it up.

We will sit and sing a lot.
We will play with my pet, Spot.
They will help to walk my pet.
Pam and Jill will not forget!
We just want to jump and run.
When I'm well, that will be fun.

This rhyme includes words your child is working with in school: words with short vowels (*sit, Pam, cup*) and words with final consonant blends (*help, jump, hand, want, toast*). Sing "My Pals" together. Think up rhyming words for the words with the final blends.

(fold here)

Name: _____

You are your child's first and best teacher!

Here are ways to help your child practice skills while having fun!

Day 1 Take turns making up sentences containing mostly words with the same short vowel sounds. For example, a short *a* sentence might be: *Tad and Max had a cat in the van.*

Day 2 Ask your child to use the words *came, know, out, she,* and *there* in sentences about doing something with a friend.

Day 3 Look for pronouns like *he, him, she, her,* and *we* in your child's favorite stories. Ask your child to tell you who each pronoun represents.

Day 4 Read a favorite story with your child. Together find the nouns in the story that name people, places, or things.

Day 5 Ask your child to draw a scene of a favorite game your child plays with a friend, such as tag. Then have your child describe to you what is happening in the picture he or she drew.

Read with your child EVERY DAY!

Circle the Pond

Materials 1 button per player, 1 penny

Game Directions

1. Place buttons on gameboard and take turns flipping a penny. Heads moves ahead two spaces, and tails moves one space.

2. When landing on a space, a player must name a word ending with the blend shown. Words may only be used once. Make a list to keep track.

3. A player unable to name a word must go back to where he or she started the turn.

4. The first player to jump into the pond wins!

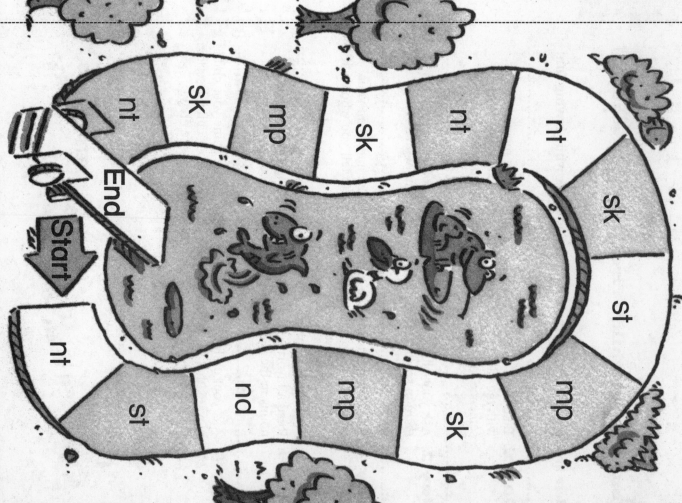

Name _____

Say the word for each picture.
Circle the letter to finish each word.
Write the letter on the line.

T**e**d **a**nd B**u**d

a e i o u
1. b ___ s

a e i o u
2. h ___ t

a e i o u
3. p ___ g

a e i o u
4. j ___ t

a e i o u
5. c ___ t

a e i o u
6. f ___ x

a e i o u
7. t ___ p

a e i o u
8. m ___ p

a e i o u
9. b ___ d

a e i o u
10. c ___ p

Notes for Home: Your child studied words with the short vowel pattern CVC (consonant-vowel-consonant) as in *ran* and *net*. **Home Activity:** Challenge your child to think of three new words that show this pattern for each vowel.

© Scott Foresman 1

Name _____

Say the word for each picture.
Circle the letters to finish each word.
Write the letters on the line.

sta**mp**

nd   nt

1. po _____

nt   st

2. fi _____

mp   nt

3. ce _____

st   mp

4. pu _____

st   mp

5. la _____

nt   nd

6. ha _____

st   nt

7. ca _____

nt   mp

8. te _____

nd   st

9. sa _____

nt   mp

10. ju _____

Notes for Home: Your child is studying final consonant blends such as *-mp, -nd, -nt,* and *-st.*
Home Activity: Ask your child to make up two sentences that each have a word with a final consonant blend.

Level 1.3

Name _____

Pick a word from the box to finish each sentence.
Write it on the line.

| came | know | out | she | there |

1. Meg _____ to the pond.

2. _____ saw a tent.

3. "I _____ that tent," said Meg.

4. "I know Dan and Lucky will be in _____ ."

5. Dan and Lucky ran _____ of the tent!

Notes for Home: This week your child is learning to read the words *came, know, out, she,* and *there.* **Home Activity:** On a piece of paper, write the first and last letters of each word. Say each word aloud and ask your child to fill in the middle letter or letters.

© Scott Foresman 1

Read each sentence.

Circle the word or words that mean the same as the underlined word.

1. Tim and Liz run fast.
   <u>They</u> want to get to the pond.

   Tim   Liz   Tim and Liz

2. Tim likes to sit by the water. <u>He</u> sees a duck.

   Tim   Liz   the duck

3. Liz sees <u>it</u> too.

   Tim   Liz   the duck

4. The duck calls out to <u>them</u>.

   Liz   the duck   Tim and Liz

5. "<u>You</u> go away!" the duck calls to them.
   Now Tim and Liz see the nest.

   Tim and Liz   the duck   the eggs

Notes for Home: Your child used words and pictures to identify the person or thing that each pronoun represents. *Home Activity:* Read the above sentences with your child. Discuss the clues he or she used to figure out each answer.

© Scott Foresman 1

A **noun** names a person, place, animal, or thing.
A noun can be in more than one part of a sentence.

The **cat** sees the **fish**.

The **dog** sees the **cat**!

Underline the nouns in each sentence.
Draw a picture to show each noun.

1. The truck holds rocks.

2. The man chops a log.

3. The frog eats a bug.

4. The bug is on the rug.

5. The black cat has a hat.

Notes for Home: Your child identified nouns in different parts of sentences.
Home Activity: Make up a simple sentence that uses two nouns, one in the naming part of the
sentence and one in the action part like those above. Ask your child to find the nouns.

Pick a word from the box to finish each sentence.
Write it in the puzzle.

came   know   out   she   there

1. Do you _____ what is in the box?

2. The frog hops _____ of the box!

3. The frog does not like it in _____ .

4. The frog _____ from the pond.

5. _____ wants to go back to her pond.

Notes for Home: Your child used newly learned vocabulary words to complete the crossword puzzle. *Home Activity:* Say each word from the box aloud, and ask your child to tell you what it means or use it in a sentence.

Name _____

Circle the nouns in each group of words.
Use them to write a sentence that makes sense.
Write the nouns on the lines.

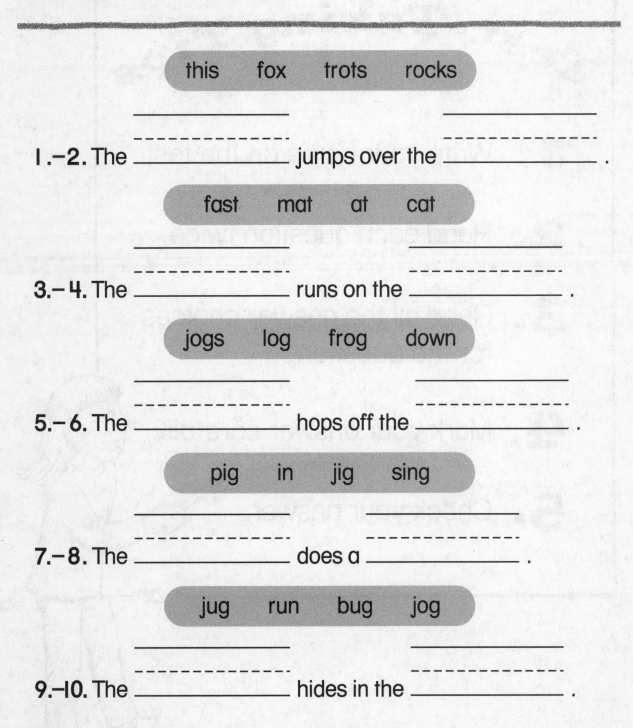

this   fox   trots   rocks

1.–2. The _____ jumps over the _____ .

fast   mat   at   cat

3.–4. The _____ runs on the _____ .

jogs   log   frog   down

5.–6. The _____ hops off the _____ .

pig   in   jig   sing

7.–8. The _____ does a _____ .

jug   run   bug   jog

9.–10. The _____ hides in the _____ .

Notes for Home: Your child reviewed nouns that appear in different parts of sentences. *Home Activity:* Together, make up sentences in which the nouns can be reversed. *(The cat is on the hat. The hat is on the cat.)* Have your child write both versions, and draw what each one describes.

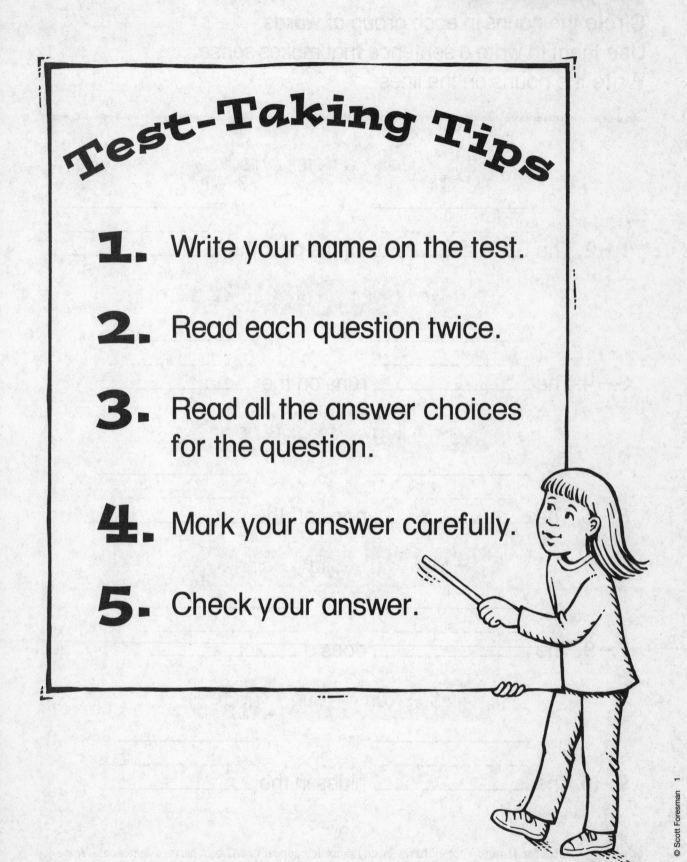

Test-Taking Tips

1. Write your name on the test.

2. Read each question twice.

3. Read all the answer choices for the question.

4. Mark your answer carefully.

5. Check your answer.

Name _____

Part 1: Vocabulary

Read each sentence.

Mark the ⬭ for the word that fits.

1. Do you _____ what time it is?
   - ⬭ who
   - ⬭ too
   - ⬭ know

2. Ana went _____ to play.
   - ⬭ out
   - ⬭ help
   - ⬭ some

3. _____ brings a ball.
   - ⬭ Our
   - ⬭ She
   - ⬭ So

4. Kim and Dan are _____ .
   - ⬭ with
   - ⬭ for
   - ⬭ there

5. Ana _____ in at two.
   - ⬭ came
   - ⬭ hold
   - ⬭ know

GO ON ➡

Part 2: Comprehension

Read each sentence.
Mark the ⬭ for the answer.

6. To Fox and Bear, the moon looked
   - ⬭ sad.
   - ⬭ red.
   - ⬭ fat.

7. As Bear sat and sat, Fox
   - ⬭ went to sleep.
   - ⬭ jumped in.
   - ⬭ played.

8. "She looked at the moon." Who is she?
   - ⬭ Fox
   - ⬭ Bear
   - ⬭ Cat

9. When the moon was gone, where did it go?
   - ⬭ in the water
   - ⬭ behind a cloud
   - ⬭ by the tree

10. What did Bear do at the end?
    - ⬭ Bear got the moon out.
    - ⬭ Bear gave Fox a pat.
    - ⬭ Bear had a nap.

Name _____

Circle the word for each picture.

black

1. block
   flock

2. slant
   plant

3. flag
   glad

4. slip
   slap

5. snug
   slug

6. sled
   fled

7. clap
   flap

8. class
   glass

Find the word that has the same beginning sound as the picture.
Mark the ⬭ to show your answer.

9. ⬭ clink
   ⬭ slam
   ⬭ like

10. ⬭ clip
    ⬭ flip
    ⬭ trip

Notes for Home: Your child reviewed words that begin with *bl, cl, fl, gl, pl,* and *sl*.
Home Activity: Have your child tell you a sentence containing several words with the same
beginning sounds. Help your child write and read the sentences. *(The slug slid down the slope.)*

fast	best	just	must	hand	and

Write the words from the box that rhyme with each picture.

1. _____   2. _____

3. _____   4. _____

Write the word from the box that rhymes with each word below.

5. last _____   6. test _____

Write the word from the box to match each clue.

7. not slow   8. better than the rest

_____   _____

_____   _____

Write the word from the box that means
the opposite of each word below.

out	came

9. went _____   10. in _____

Notes for Home: Your child spelled words that end with *st* and *nd* and two frequently used
words: *out, came*. **Home Activity:** Have your child use these words to tell you a story about
two friends. Help your child to write and read the finished story.